Pennsylvania Collection Agency

Michael Burkard

New Issues Poetry & Prose

A Green Rose Book
Selected by David Dodd Lee

New Issues Poetry & Prose
The College of Arts and Sciences
Western Michigan University
Kalamazoo, MI 49008

First Edition, 2001

ISBN: 1-930974-00-0 (paperbound)

Library of Congress Cataloging-in-Publication Data:
Burkard, Michael
Pennsylvania Collection Agency/Michael Burkard
Library of Congress Catalog Card Number (00-132523)

Art Direction:	Tricia Hennessy
Design:	Todd Marcy
Production:	Paul Sizer
	The Design Center, Department of Art
	College of Fine Arts
	Western Michigan University
Printing:	Courier Corporation

Pennsylvania Collection Agency

Michael Burkard

New Issues

WESTERN MICHIGAN UNIVERSITY

Also by Michael Burkard

In a White Light
None, River
Ruby for Grief
The Fires They Kept
Fictions from the Self
My Secret Boat
Entire Dilemma
Unsleeping

for Nancy Mitchell

It is always so early inside here, before the fork in the road, before the irrevocable decision. Thanks for this life! Still, I miss alternatives. All sketches want to become real.

—Tomas Tranströmer, "The Blue House"
(translated by Samuel Charters)

Contents

"Amends"

It's 11.9 miles to Mardela Springs.
The public school's a left away from
the town which is too small to be called
a town.

Past the school and heading
south is a road which
immediately kisses country,
a large pond there

with a house
beside it.
The shadows
in the fall morning
make a wing beside the house.

The students are tired.
It's Monday. It doesn't seem
to matter what day, most of the time
they're tired.

In the early fall dark
the road whispers to the pond.
"Amends." School is out, no one hears. In 216
the janitor replaces a fluorescent light.
He drops a screw from ten steps up.

The school is so quiet it hears the drop.
The school and the road begin their talk.
Soon the pond joins in.
"Amends."

Pennsylvania Collection Agency

A Primitive Plane

When she announced from her list
she had no gate for Flight 884
I wondered if it meant: there will be
no gate in heaven for this flight.

Memory's killed me all my life
and not *it's not*.

One shadow loans
another its cloak: the latter
is assigned a journey on a boat
and needs a double:
one for the deck
and one for the split shadow
down on the water
that no one will probably
ever see.

Shadows are more exact
than I.

There's a replica of a famous couple's porch
in a small town near Tupelo.
A memory might be more exact:

memory might know the shadows
which accompanied the porch in the first place—
though memory'd never say so.

I'm Jack,
you're John,
he's Clarence.

We're on a road in Mississippi.
It's raining.
We've talked a long time,
now we're quiet.

One of us is wondering if we're heading
to a gate.
Another is very blue, even in the face.
The third is watching the road
and the shadows raining there.

my brother dreams

the dark secret of the landscape in the dream
is failure: this is the court of last resort: my brain:
i am innocent of all charges, i protest, my brain
does not acknowledge a legitimate protest.

in the dream the dunes are beside a lake:
a conductor conducts me back and forth
along the lake's edge: i am in an open
gondola which is doubling for a train.

other writers are correct, i am incorrect: i am
guilty as charged for being incorrect: for using "i"
when "i" wasn't i, for telling the truth and lying:
my brother dreams even more than i do:

evergreens, topical maps, ambushes: he dreams
these and other dreams he says: i am going to sleep
in a room kept normally for my brother:
he is a secret if there ever was one.

my sister is missing from this conspiracy of silence:
the door to her and her husband's room is
missing like a light: they live in a house large
enough for an extended family: the missing

ones would even have a seat: the clouds you can
witness from one of many windows:
the sea you can smell from the outside:
the funeral for my aunt is tomorrow:

if ever i had a sense there is life
beyond a coffin it is now: lelia
is not the lelia in the coffin,
she is already gone, departed for who

knows where: somehow i sense the energy
is intact, though i am not anxious to try it:
lelia will be buried in Evergreen
Cemetery, near there once my hands were

washed accidentally by the moon:
this is true. one of those moments which
pervade even a silence. in what
i will for one moment's sake call

the silence of the soul i want to say:
i have often dreamt of the burial
ground of my ancestors: i am visiting,
i am there. the township is full

of water. i do not want to leave
in the dream for i have touched
no one. i cannot believe this:
i have been there and have not touched.

my sister's house is in a natural
night dark tonight: you can smell
the sea: the sea smells the night:
the house is at peace against the sea.

life is intact.

Because

Gogol (his namesake)
spoke the other day with a famous writer
who'd given up. The moon arches over the silver trees
—as if the trees
had given up the ghost.

The writer had to whisper:
"It just doesn't work. Word's don't. Silences don't."
And when "don't" was struck the second time
she looked Gogol straight in the eye, as if to say
"Say they don't."

The moon can complicate:
it is difficult to see the night bird
range against the moonlight,
both even at their brightest
are a shade too dim.

The writer said she'd had a plan once, of traveling,
traveling in a country she didn't know,
becoming a stranger again
to everything and all but herself.
She lacked, she said, a coherent plan.

The moon must be coherent
because it waits for the almost eternal time
the sun will show
and from what angle.

Perhaps a secret of the moon in space is that in one real sense
there is no absolute perspective.

The Letter

1

When he was twenty-one he thought of almost every country,
but he hadn't any manner of writing about them,
which was what he wanted to do,
so in secret (as if someone cared) he named one "Cruelty"
and at that called it quits.

2

He took to writing letters.
They were never letters about God or Death, the only two real topics
he cared about. So he approached these shyly, abruptly, awkwardly.
The approaches always came across as jokes.

3

When you are embarrassed about your life
find a new direction. Burn the letter never sent
so that a dramatic new beginning occurs.
Tell no one except your own life.
Look up, but stop talking to the sky.

4

I have made my mailman my higher power.
This is a foolish thing to do.
The sun is a metal. The sun is bright.
It is going to rain anyway, today, tomorrow, at night.
I am going to write a letter about death and god,
I am going to be naive, if that is what it calls for.

5

Unspoken, so much is unspoken: the tree, the night, the silence.
Everyone wants me to be someone else! Except at night!
At night I am free, I know the night wants me, wants me as is.
Two of the larger lessons in my life: a comic book cover, smoke from
   a gun, my confusion

about the man's face behind the smoke. Too: being hammered by a stick
  for taking down my pants at the age of five. I was in the bushes,
    she was in the bushes.
My mother, alas, was not in the bushes, but soon enough . . .

I feel now I have written for some other reason, some other motive
than giving the gift the poem brought.
I founded a major portion of my adult life on some other reason,
  almost like the smoke
I just talked about, almost confused, but not enough.
And now there is a revolution: my own. Destination small but
  unknown, the journey
and not the reputation.

I was going to read Anna Karenina in order to hide again.
I hid in that story as Anna for six years or more.
And before her story another, and another . . .
It is as if there was always another story to die in.

I am dead, I is dead, I wish I wish upon a star
and a voice returns always in silence, and now I wish in silence.
I have led my own life to the end.

I saw myself huddling in the winter with a few local friends.
The town has died—something, though not time, has passed it by.
Something irrevocable, though I don't know what it is.
Maybe it is the literal metaphor of the nuclear shadow: there is an
  overwhelming base
here, and the bombers practice by day and night.

By name and by night someone else is giving up.
The stars are high, the sea is deep. The night feels like a shadow.

Seen

Seen the uncaring realms
of old hillsides too often
to care. Heard the appropriated life

once too often: I did let them
own me, didn't I? Heard your wail
too often to return.

Strange town called
Mariaville. A lake,
creepy house across the street from

and facing the lake. No one there.
Followed by a stranger town
called Minaville.

Too often the name is
a strange star: where will
you find me, o where.

Loved the evening
and loved by it.
Evening enough it died.

Love you as family, as
no one there. As strange,
which you are.

The Moon Is Free

Here is a story broken in flight.
Here the daughter leaves home with a necktie.
Here the brother considers suicide but doesn't act.
Here is the memory of the bird they shot at.
Here the daughter remembers it sadly.
Here the brother remembers with guilt.

Guilt and sadness inhabit the self remembering.
The future is a stick
which is found on a road
by a small woman with three eyes.

At last, at last
do not remember what she was saying.
All I know is I heard her voice.

A candle is shaking its fist at death.
The flame momentarily is wild.
Because they are lovers and have looked forward to this moment
    with the candle she considers the shaking unfair.
It isn't tender enough.

If she knew it was death
she would have another feeling.

If she knew it was death
she would have another feeling.

Death is sudden.
Death doesn't require an act.

The moon is free and kisses the daughter, regardless of the fact that
    she has left home
—the moon kisses the brother regardless of his guilt.

The moon is so sudden you can taste it.
All you have to do is open your mouth.

Because the sea has a historical knowledge of both bird and death
the sea comprehends the sudden quality of the moon.

At last the sun shines on a cliff
where a woman is sitting on a stone.

The nameless bird listens from death.
From its perspective of death
it is giving birth to the woman.
She is not alone.
She has never been alone.

The Gift

for my sister

Today you are 36. No: 48. No!
38. George Cleveland was born in '33.
Mae in '39. Do you still see
when George and Mae took us to the hull
of "the dark ship" in the deep woods
above Carleton? How no one ever knew
how the hull got there? Didn't we dance for
a few moments before we feared we might upset
a spirit?   But then I am as you have said

obsessed with the past. Well
I don't know if I would call it an obsession
now. Still and enough it was. I had
no present. I had one but no way in,
no way out, no way out there it seemed
to walk with anyone except a crooked
figure from back there.

On a day of snow all is said
and done which was said the day before.
I was reading a story of religious conversations
last night and even though I am not
among them I saw us touching
the dark ship. Did it touch us? Isn't
"touched" another way of being "mental"?
Where there are ruins there is a fire
even if it is invisible fire.

The fire never goes out.
It burns beyond being in a dimension to the side.
I prefer to say "side" since there is no
up or down, in or out. Maybe side
and near or far. They have some quiet
which the galaxy could use.
I give you this as a gift.

Each of Them Icons

1

o what is tired
but an old old song?
a major act of terrorism
flies like the night
flies to the moon—
even the songs of these dead
are becoming horribly familiar
old songs . . .

she was hit by two
or three bullets
as she crossed from the church
to her car . . .

this is what stevenson said
when I was young:

the old man had never gone
to church and finally went
in a wheelchair with a bible
in his hands, and somehow the story went
he got up to pray

(whoever got up
to pray?)

collapsed and died
with the bible across his heart . . .

the finish was the detail
that he would burn in hell

and I assented yes
believing some dark condition
in the story

convinced never
knowing why

2

with the moon waning
and the lamp still on
in the house: why did my bones
believe stevenson? what darkness
in that false story was a life?

—one doesn't know.
one knows the sun
and the fact of bullets
in the sun—one knows

there seems no reaching for spirit
which could amend—

if it is a basically orderly
universe

the sun
and the window are one

the lamp and the bullet
are one

or two or three or five:
an omission to five

and butchie stevenson is out there
in this world tonight

either dead
or alive

3

John, there is an instrument
of time

neither you nor I ever decided
was relevant to the dream:

time
in the sense of song
for itself, light upon day,
dark upon night,

—I don't know how else
to describe it.
I am afraid to say:
"I believe in the dream per se."

Just as it is,
just as it was,
just as when I am empty of night
when I haven't dreamt.

But I am afraid.
They will say this isn't real.
hearing them, I will say
this isn't real . . .

and hearing those voices one last time
will be enough to kill me.
I am saying out loud tonight god help me
for the broken places I have made.

4

And you who
know me
yet deny me
I feel from this lost place

where the words I have written
no longer understand for me
no longer bare any fact
any song except that they took place,

occurred through
me but are not mine . . .
for mine has changed as the time
was by the rock—

the fire had arrived at the rock one time
and I fled, not at all wanting to flee
but fled—and I knew I would not have been harmed
for the words of someone else

had written it.
I am not complete
apart from you I am less than that
—I whisper across the face of the night sky

and need you to hear me,
want this inutterable distance
to die physically, to break too
so I may never leave you.

This is not a poem, it is not owned
it is not loaned from another voice—
nothing I have said has ever been a poem
a category—I know not.

What does this make me?
Loved ones abound in this place of "home"
I am now in—and yes—
as you said it is devastating—

I cannot accept their literal
silences—my mother
devastates me, my father,
I let him rule

—we always let him rule
and we never said so
which is a twisted fact
which can make a life

feel like debris
because of the twists
of silence—everyday when I move
throughout this house I feel as if I

am watching my brother
as if I am him in body—
one family has digested me for so many years
I must fear all family—

as if the function of family
without anyone responsibly knowing
was to digest, eat alive,
take the spirit from one

and choke it . . .
and I am to blame for even citing here
in words no one will see—
the blame feels like a ship one could see

with fear returning again to the harbor,
horizon flat, water still
and here comes the deadly ship.
Jesus, it just left . . .

When I was living as a drunk
in Provincetown there was a time
in the morning when I would
accidentally wake

climb forward from the bed
and leaning out see 4 or 5
of the fishing boats heading
out—I could feel the cold

and their masts looked
darker than they were
because the sun had not yet
risen but was already giving

some light and at those
moments I wanted to live
more than I ever had
and I would sit in silence

which I wanted to last
an entire life.

5

One can't watch boats
an entire life—one can't
watch the sea an entire life:
these words were spoken
by a deadly ghost I call "mine"—
and "yours" and all the other deadly explosions
from the sun—but the sun is far enough away
to eliminate the accuracy of "deadly"—which
applies only in some fiction
which approaches it.
"One"—the fiction of my life,
my silence—need a sun
upon a horizon which will
eliminate the kind of darkness
which issues from my head.
The heads of state have issued
enough darkness for each of us
a thousand-fold. And also
each of us as "one"
issuing said darkness
when the light seems to die somewhere
and not accepting dark we desperately
fight "one"—
this one, that one . . .

6

One is both a house
and a dream. In the house
one dreams, in the dream one
constructs one's own house.
Each is too owned.

7

In the dream the fact was
he was making love to women—
the logic was men will therefore have
to be made love to as well—immediately.

He sensed in the dream
a controlling fear,
that men had to follow
women. Then there

was a friend named
Mary, beside her
old old women on
a plain, waiting,

waiting. And in talking
with Mary he found
she too had changed.
Was more one

or one again
as somewhere
she had been,
alluded to.

8

As well as Mary
there is an ancient song
she sang, and he can hear it

by the rock against the sky:
the song is the icon,
the houses we thought
songs, the houses we
dreamed we thought
songs—each of them
icons, almost as
the brittle evening star
is an icon in the
desert sky—brittle as
he perceives the slightest
wobbling in the light—
it is in the brittle
air, a desert song
not unlike Vallejo's
black stone, white stone—
an ancient song which
seems to have all to do
with the universe.

9

The desert is not a far piece
from the sea—in a few geological years

one floor will inherit the other—
the houses will vanish

as historical figures vanish—
a species will erupt

so far down the road
it is difficult if not impossible

to vanish. To say the image will
have the weight of a fact

is to say one will not vanish—
to say each will be the other

is to say one will not vanish—
and I do not say that.

But on the road to that far road
I say one is the other, the spiritual

the real, the real the spiritual—
the fact is

the image, the image the fact—
this is the house, the desert.

10

The house is a sea
is a desert.

The moon at sea
is the house at sea.

The moon shines upon
the desert floor

—the sea contends
with the moon and sea.

It is night
and the sea seems to shine

as the fishing boats
head out.

The desert is silent
except for a sea of stars

which are almost loud
in their clarity.

The night is a sea.
The house is quiet.

One is everywhere,
everywhere feels one.

House, desert, sea:
each is already

within eternal space.
Space. Space.

The form is an icon
of space.

What I Threw into the Grave

how can I help it
good moonlight, bad rain,
Carl, dusk, picture
of Carl at dusk with
Mona in the background
partially thumbed out,
an unnecessary angel,
the necessary mop,
shadow of the mop,
ten pages covered
in typescript with
the words I'm leaving

this museum / that museum
the cruel sea the mariner's
decoy I stole while housesitting
verbatim, apparition,
a twilight, piece of meteor
from a childhood summer
in Yarmouth, Nova Scotia,
a pencil to draw the
way to you and the way
back, "we work with
life therefore because
of that work we are

closer to death,"
socks, a fear
of drowning, a love
for staying on the
open road, a boundary
(just on the outside
chance you'll need a
boundary), help, leaves
(a few), 5 red bottles,
a small window,
an evening, good
rain, cruel sea.

A Fire in the Arrow

Someone's trying to imitate Cole's voice. It's an ad
for marriage. Take this down as an ad: the Father's
photograph, the years he served, and pasted over it is
a picture of the woman he fooled around with.
The rectory went kaput for awhile, there's a year gap
between his end dates and the date of the next
and current Rector. The couple survived.
I knew the husband years ago and thought the photograph of Father

resembled her husband if her husband had been a slightly
different life: a little more inward, scholarly, crazed in the eyes
but facially intact.

There's a fire in the arrow tonight. So much snow is falling
no one is getting through. A couple I'm not dying to see but feel
I must has just moved into what I consider a haunted house:
their lights were on all over the place. Two deaths two decades
ago literally took place inside the house. Their marriage is like
    the beautiful face of a star:

a river and an emptiness dwell in it simultaneously. The face of a star
which thinks at night there is something new in the world if only I can
    find it.

A small forest sighs behind the house. A little tree sighs from the
    weight of the snow.
The Father still feels misplaced in the parish in a smaller city.

he forged

the letters so well that none of us saw the light, a kind
of occupational blindness aided him too: one was: we have
many reservations about your inflationary theory: stop: he stopped:
it was I who handed the letter read through the whole affair
and so spotted the despite/acceptance at the end. and he was
appropriately overjoyed with just enough reservation to convince
even the out-of-season-daffodils attempting to survive
in the hospital foyer.

a single lone esoteric memory: didn't we smash the doors
down to his house trying to get in, assured by the silence he

hid within: and wasn't the place as empty of him as silence? and
this: "this" is only about "this"—there can be no other aspect to
the story, thus referential is a terribly misleading term: his
disease referred to whom? the psychological terminology named
like a clinical dream some condition no one of us could put
a finger on. and when the anniversary of his firing from Yale arrived
none of us despite our knowledge of other terminal anniversaries
guessed: he chose

a respectful overdose of fire and silence in which to leave
he didn't let anyone know and no one had to share
the fire with him

Her Healing

"It is against the death, the night—
it is against all forms lovely or strange.
There isn't much it is not against.

H
I
J

Even they it is against.
Harmless letters, but they form a character
for meaning, and being a form
it is therefore against them."

To depart from one life to the next—doesn't this seem peculiar?
This sense of departure?

"It is very peculiar, yet we cannot quite say why.
Moment to moment there is a departure, not a moment occurs
on this world without departure. It is so simple as to be ignored
but in ignoring it many have found their own departures lacking,
which they never are."

The woman then told of her healing.
But all the while she talked she looked so sick, sounded so
    far from touch.
I even felt there were moments of bold arrogance
coupled with a sense that she had said all this before:

"I found my past inside a dead starling.
My past was a boat. I boarded the boat
and sailed to a life of birds, all birds,
I was welcomed as a starling.
In their world they are constantly defending ours
with songs and codes and jabbers. Their sadness, and that is the
closest sign I can call it, reflects ours: they see us
as having misunderstood them also, and there are barriers and reefs
in the real world and beneath which will guarantee a continuation.

I am taken to a reef and released.
My forgetfulness is handed to me as my other hand
—years will transpire and I will know a place called memory.
Gradations of memory will accumulate.
I will have this sense as I am having now
that the present transpired before,

where everyone had forgotten me,
and every river and every tree I sang from
denied me, denies I ever sang.
All songs have an overlapping latitude,
I wade into one and know the river is singing the song too,
the black tree sings the song, the yellow stone sings the song
beside the lonely light.

The boat transpires
in a harbor where thousands of starlings
harbor at dusk in the nearby trees.
Sound of a wave clapping on another wave,
sound of the song breathing at the water.

As an evasion memory hasn't healed a wave,
but memory is hanging at the harbor wanting to remember me."

How Much of the Life

"My life"—Gorky's said so too.
My life: defended by humiliations.
Tonight, waiting for rain to fall, see the life
marked by one humiliation after another.
Humiliated by men. Before they were men, boys.
Never knowing until this precise moment how much of the life
is marked in my mind by these.

Took Jung's suggestion and asked anima
What are you up to now?
A picture formed, then another, another—
punches thrown at me, clothes torn off, names called
by bigger boys, losing fistfights, watching my brother lose fistfights,
being hit in the head by a large stone, a can, a large shingle (directly
upon the esophagus), two men also wanting to beat on me because
    I would not go to Vietnam.
The doctor/boss berating me, neighborhood chums berating me,
    collegiate chums berating me.

The list goes on. Did not know how unconsciously I mark
    everything with
because of these and—honestly—countless more.

I Made a Tree

I liked the impersonality:
they changed the sheets, the towels, they
may have changed the lighting, the place itself was so impersonal
I wouldn't have seen it.

I did not see much of the sky.
I saw very little of night
except the night I could see inside myself
—I was inside so very much.
I did hear a bell again, this time it rang
from a river nearby, or the simple road
beyond the simple river.

Even a true journey risks very serious mistakes:
I might be crying at destiny without even knowing it . . .
do you wonder if there is such a destiny which longs
for us also . . . a destiny which describes the past and the future
as futile, hopeless, trusting all the while that someone will realize
the present is missing and befriend it
—and by befriending the present give destiny the kiss
it has so longed for?

It had a rail to it:
I climbed to the room each evening and did not leave.
From the window I could see the river
dropping away to the east.
Beyond that a small bridge,
the beginning of a road.

I made a tree. I didn't know quite where it belonged.
That didn't stop me.

January 24, 1986

(moonset)

Oh on a certain morning I want to guarantee
my father did not stop. The neighbor stopped and on a certain day
I failed to say hello to him, he did not
speak to me for weeks. He was a crazy neighbor. Wound up dying

at a railroad crossing in Shelburne, Nova Scotia, with his wife.
His not speaking is not connected to his death, although I feel
now there was a time when I may have put the two together
    knowingly or not.
I placed death close to the most personal events,

the ones I called queer, where I either reflected myself to myself or
simply saw this person I labeled fool, me, asshole. It got so bad
that at the end I would drive around in the truck by myself
and call myself an asshole: for I even had a kind of rhapsody

wondering how they did not hear the train in fog, although fog
explains it, wondering why the trackside graves were made by
locals for them, one cross even hung the remains of a straw hat,
and there was even a mound and a cross for their dog Charlie.
And wondering

what they ate for dinner the night before, if Raddy tried to beat
the train. And why my father took photographs of the site then
later destroyed the slides. Oh he was a quiet one my father and I
don't know if the quietness lives on or not. I don't know if I can
talk about it.

I can write around it, I know that, but to talk to it would be like
saying Yes, Death, I have some fear of you, yet, I cannot pretend.
Yes, Life, Yes, Death, I want to love myself for I have waited
so long to love or talk as simply as that.

January 24, 1986

(noon)

Her name was Lola but it wasn't. Her name was Dolores,
she changed it herself to Lola, so when I told you her name
was Dolores it was my small way of not telling you anything
which was none of your business. And yes I loved not because I
knew her but because I did not, and love is easy and anything
I want to call it from that distance. I can call birds love, the ring
love, the moon the father and the name the loan. The distance is
a fact of not knowing, trying to draw near to that which isn't
known.

Because I did not know her I made a room for us and we lived
there about 2 minutes a week, x 7, this was about all the time she
took.
So love is fast and rapid and fixed even in a close calculation
from a distance / locale of not knowing. I do not know her now.
If someone is waiting for me she is standing right here or up the
road at work, red work, or if it's a he a friend in life he is sick at
home and had last night to sleep 13 hours.
Even my coaxing I will chauffeur cannot get him

out and I don't blame him and even my lunging that she quit red
work didn't work. So be it. I know them, I do not know them.
They are close. I see I know them in a fact of things: an unburnt
moon, a sky to talk to, the view of the night sky between the pines
when I walk into his yard. I know I don't know. Maybe I would
like England as he suggests, maybe I could like the sea more as she
has talked to me. We'll see. The three of us. In some journey with
boundaries and a lack of boundaries as we travel up the road.

Night Interior

looking at van Gogh's
night room I see I never saw
this feeling of Macbeth and this
tidal red which offsets the tidal
green. No one is shooting billiards
and they look remote, or faceless
as I felt when looking tonight

toward the south I saw the night
light on the wire-mesh and for
a moment saw a seascape town
of lights and had to turn again
to be sure what I was saying wasn't
being seen:

        would rather be a lamp
in this night interior than to
have to face that bridge again,
heading south toward the sea but
as far as I am concerned away
from the sea, headed to where
all those ships washed up
or
    stayed down, like a letter
in a bottle at the bottom
of a sea. There must be many
such letters.

    The Russian oil on
canvas of Midday, Summer, 1917
makes much more sense: in this
there is no below or wreck
that the sea makes: the valleys are
tilted in a simple perspective,

life is mid-life with
phases taking place: a coffin
  carried, a wagon hauling two

semi-lovers speaking for
a moment in a field. There
is more to this than meets
the eye and there is a village
and two white silos far far
off / is this the village

ridden off from in a later one,
A Fantasy, with the red horse red
and even the woman pointing it
out in a kind of red, a robe:

like the lamp the village
sleeps with on a single night

when the rider has ridden off
to a world unknown. The world
is unknown. You can almost
smell the skin of the horse's teeth,

the air at night in the hills,
the grass under the beautiful dark
night.

Love. Petro-Vodkin also did one
called The Couple. They are sitting
on a quiet precipice. In Night
Interior van Gogh signs only
Vincent at the lower right.

Katya

I got away with alcohol for maybe ten years.
Then it became a counterweight, then only a weight.
My father, who I grew up feeling was a large bore,
tried warning me, I can see that now.
I wish a ghost of him and my mother could
climb from the sky one night,
for just enough time . . .
I keep a small wooden heart where I've written their names,
I keep it beside my favorite window, a token for them.

When I escaped from Hungary I believed I was free—
little did I know I carried my other enemy, alcohol, with me.
It is deceitful, an increasingly bad lover with whom I became
more and more obsessed. Quietly at first, privately.
Then loudly, openly.

I did not know the end was near. I lived in a house
across from a cemetery. I had taken a temporary teaching job.
I stood one Saturday morning
looking out to the cemetery. It was an early spring day,
the sky was blue. I felt such a prison inside me
the house was a prison, the window, the dead, the sky.
The house's street number was the same number—907—of the first
house I had stayed in in America. And now,
on this Saturday-prison-morning,
I degraded myself for ever having thought something wonderful or
significant would occur for me in this house-of-907.

It never dawned on me that perhaps the scotch in my hand
    was the prison.
Drinking it, as I saw and felt these prisons, I never blamed
    my difficult lover alcohol.
Not then, not even when I first stopped.

Perhaps another kind of end is near, well, if it is, I prefer seeing it
from this side. I want to close by telling you
a small detail from a dream I recently had.

I am in Budapest again. My mother and father are standing beside
     two
yellow urns. There is a bird's nest in one of the urns, the one
beside my father. The bird's nest is warning us
the city is on fire. I am wondering 'Where is the bird to the nest?'
My mother and father vanish and I and the two urns are inside
     a house,
a house inside the city, but there is a clear, overwhelming sense in the
     dream
the house itself will secure my freedom.
I leave the house and turn around. It is the house-of-907.

and, and

One man said his dreams ended when his drinking began.
Some of mine ended at that too, and some began.

In a life of comparison there is always a dream,
however inappropriate, however grand, however out of harmony
with the sense of one, two, three—the ordinary day near

the ordinary harbor, the ordinary sun against the ordinary sea.
And when the lives went out to sea no one went with them,

until one got sick with the comparison, and resentment entered,
   anger
entered, despair entered. They entered with a silence, like a face
conquering a dream, becoming another face, becoming a thunder

from a past inhabited by a desert, a sky, a rock.
So when one man said his dreams ended when his drinking began

I took exception. I regret having to say again I do not know.
I do not know exactly at which moment anything begins or ends,
I do not know exactly when my life waned. It waned,

that is enough. My life compared like an endless clock,
it is exhausting to walk years and years not being yourself,

knowing that you are not yourself but walking again and again.
The faces did not matter, a face could have asked me to stop
and I could not stop. Life was *and, and*.

One of my friends was called The Windmill. I was The Spartan.
We were both exhausted.

Later She Said I Was Like a Sparrow with Cash in His Pocket

for Sara

Some people did well in school because
of a relationship to paper, the work space
of the paper . . . provided a comfort
like a shadow of yourself
the moon or sun brings back
without asking your consent

Regardless, I quit math. Excellently
I watch other people doing math,
it gives me a chill, a constant—
the largest momentary thrill's when
someone mutters I hate math
but proceeds neatly after a moment

She wears a watch on her foot
a bracelet with a sparrow for a
charm. A child said
that when she first met me I
looked like a vulture, later she said
I was like a sparrow with cash in his pocket

If either is even nearly true
the young child knows like a
night which may have known me
or any of us. They do know us.
Like the houses and the trees and the road
they are keeping a very strict account.

Moon to a Far Planet

1

I would now swear
I do know little of love.
I have what could only be called a
singular love,
one bird instead of two,
Sweetheart, enjoy yourself when you detrain,
I am proceeding to another station. Not inferior,
not superior. Just another.

When this thing called love
shoves beyond the singular I lose it.
One year I lost an illicit magazine, a pair of pants, a rope
and the old one dollar suitcase which contained them.
    Attempts to trace them
were nil. My attempts at love are for better or worse
not so untraceable. Unlike the meteors which have sometimes
    answered me
they have left tracks across the sky. There are many tracks
across the sky, I know, but mine
are there too.

The I is as autobiographical as I make it.
It is not for you to make it,
nor are we to decide what is believable and what is not.
This will take care of itself.
I have sat in this one particular station waiting for the train cars
    to couple
and uncouple. I have been traveling to/from perhaps 3 different
    loves
in three different silent countries
in 3 different shades of green with white.
I have sat alone and with strangers. Sometimes I have taken up
    2 seats.
I have never sat with anyone I've known.

I am not very good at being bad.
I have no content other than that given me.
Still I doubt. If the towns between the trees were to explode
I would have nothing. They are my honesty, as the night after day
     and day after night are.

2

It is the amount of all the small moments which seem to fall
neither into night nor day. It is all that is unsaid.
It is the unburnt desire to bring the same quality of love
     to more than one at once.

The desire to be the city
and not the sea.
The desire to be the satellite
and not the trolley.
The desire to be the subway
and not, god forbid, the automobile.
Especially the white one with tinted glass, which seems to come
     out of nowhere
and an average but indiscreet looking woman climbs inside.
This kind of singular fact astonishes me as much as my singular
     love.

The singular love is not biological enough.
It is not sun enough.
It has too often related a version of unhappiness.
It is loved halfly for the utter laughter it produces while its
     other half
ranges toward the abject.
It returns to childhood too much. At first with amusement (the
     THREE of us shoveled
the stars back into the snow)
and then with the lonesome: I felt so alone. I sang alone. Etc.
It was thin and frail and overcompensated with weightlifting
     the outside
and burden carrying the inside.
The heart is so tired it may go out.

Above all: it scolds itself too much.
This singular love needs to have its hands tied.

A final note: I am absolutely convinced there is no translation
    which can render
Tolstoy's ending Anna's life with sympathy.I don't think he knew
    what to do with her,
that he was very angry and impatient with her and wanted to put her out.
    It doesn't work: he
himself away, him and his singular love.

3

Exactly as the train heads west instead of north
snow is everywhere.

No one is arguing about the discovery of Miranda (moon to a far planet).
One man is retiring and this is his last trip.

I don't know where I am going
or why.
I don't know what to say.

I won't see much of the night tonight
I won't see your face.

I probably won't argue with anyone
or complicate.

You said to me how different the houses at night by the sea
are, I think you also meant houses anywhere. And my feeling was
    yes, yes,
maybe they do keep watch, do something or just be
something that would never occur to anyone.
I take wild stabs at guessing and someone might say I personify
    too much
but I have this inescapable feeling everything is trying to give us back

to them and to us, and that the gift
is simply to be.

That we end but we don't end.
That I am the stranger that I have always been.
That we are all beautiful strangers.

My Mother Orders a Children's Book

All the rain is exhausted from so much falling.
My mother orders a children's book to replace the book
which is lost. If the rain cries anymore
I will sell the house and become another one.

In the phantoms of the heart
is the harbor of a youth,
and the night comes on
when love least expects.
A city begins and ends,
a face effaces itself
before any moment is translated.
And the ships rock furiously in the waves.

My mother has climbed a hundred steps
but never these, never this shadow, never this sun,
never this high ending up against love.
Where nothing at all seemed untrue.
Where she believes the house is mine,
fraught with red questions, white sentences,
voices crossing with rain.

This is true: I have never been home.
The name is an infinity of space
I am in, I have never left.
The face tries to leave again and again,
but it cannot.

It Is Quite Red

My mother was right—
the sunset is red

though an hour ago
when she said it was red

it was at that time
a pale pale yellow—

and now an hour by
it is quite red

—next to the elm
there's a broken wing

the flight ends there
with the dark

—my mother
does not end

—it is perverse
this lack of endings

in the world
at large

and in the sky
where said

finds its way
across the stars

Nijinsky

My faith in man is renewed:
we walk back to the well
to pull the voice out:
it's cold down here,
I'm beginning to memorize
algebraic tables, or watch
the well stones as if this
is the only world now, the only
universe, and how is it to
be a universe from stone,
or recall with equal amounts
of forgiveness and hatred
the day I was lowered
from a bridge, so young
to be so lowered.
We lower the rope and the voice
gets clearer: a thief had
returned to settle an
illegal score. The old
mother is still tied up in the house
we hear and the voice runs off

—mother, I'm out, I'm free.

To Maria

He doesn't know what the story of love will look like either
although he keeps saying he knows.

The sky today is the sky to a fault,
it even sounds
like the geese which fly across,
but the sky's honking warns us: know everything,
still you will not know the flap in the heart.

He, the gigantic artist, wrote:

"The mind is the hinge the heart requires, otherwise the door to the
    heart,
as simple sounding as it is, shall never open it. The heart shall not
open without the mind."

Here is a bloodly picture of a lake and trees:
the trees seem painted slowly, the lake might not be a lake
except the trees seem reflected there, in red.

I wish the gigantic artist would mind his own business.
You and I, Maria, accept that people are only people,
geese only geese. I'm sure a billion or so else have too.
Where are they this morning—I just want to find someone
so I can wring his neck.

In lieu of someone I will wring myself. I will concentrate only
    upon my fault.
Only—is any one of us only,
trees—only, only hours

when the secret gift our childhood buried itself deep within, when
    we
witnessed the burial but did not realize a living spirit was being
    buried

within us, as we wanted to bury a toy in a cave forever.
And we are our own cave, only

we demand access with the key of the adult, the wary,

and the child will only open to a key from another child.
This is why my love fails.

This is why we feel so ruined
—let's invite the gigantic artist to dinner.

Night Mirror

Brought her on the road
through the same town
same hillside as another
brought me years ago—

my favorite slope of a
barn and two used
silos and the road taking
a final sharp turn

above it—the mind can
be such a careless thing,
thing lent, returned like
a stale heart or a

night mirror (that's what
the bad dream's called)—tonight
before dying off in her face
I told her the story

of this hill—wound like
a sky from a too distant
past—the sky seen and felt
in the mind's eye but also

dwarfed by "I."
"I" wants to smell
the hill, hear rain on
the road, invoke the scene

which her night mirror
loans me—financial terms
of the hillside, broke,
lent, rented with rain—

yet that hillside is the same
and the two drive there
heading south this time away
from the town into the sky—

so much is the night in
you it dwarfs even my
night—but then I've had
enough of my night—

Pennsylvania Collection Agency

The way he behaved could also be described
by saying that he kept me inside of him . . .

Tomorrow night he won't be here.
The report will say he is "overdue."
A car will climb almost as steep as the evening moon
seen from the bridge above the prison.

A woman is reading books for a living.
If she has ever suffered loss she won't tell you
she will tell the books, and tonight she is telling Dostoevsky's
The Idiot, the chapter of the guillotine to be exact

—to be more exact she is crying, she has stayed beside the octaves
    of the fictive
her whole life. It isn't a bad life, it's just that the boundaries have
    collapsed,
like the past collapses
when there is nothing left except the past.

Rovee Bovers, Boomer, Sweet Pea: cats and a daffodil
he has loved. And when he turns to his boundary he finds a head,
sadly he finds a head, and he believes it is
his own head. This is a typically mistaken perception which has
    been allowed to breathe

for centuries. It is no more his head than it is the sun's, the sea's,
    the book
she is suffering with under a lamp. It is as much her head as his.
    Or fire's
or moon's or bridge's. When he crosses that boundary between
    death and love
he may again witness the time he and two others visited the artist
    who was suffering

in bed. The artist was paranoid enough to believe they were his
    enemies. The artist
behaved in a way which could only be described as
momentarily having no boundary. None of them did.
And there was a small fire somewhere
burning for each of them they thought
as three of them drove back to the city.

The Pictures of Maria

They make me want to tell you a dream
in which I was living
in the house from my childhood,
the house with the people all around,
the house before we left imperceptibly for the desert,
which was a shock, a house there
but a shock nevertheless.

They make me want to tell you a woman
rented and married me and from the room
which was mine I watched for her
as drops of water collected at the paws of cats and dogs,
and I was distressed for the flickering light
accentuated the collection,
and my wife never came to visit or to see what I saw.

Pennsylvania Collection Agency

Burkard

Hotel Tropicana

It wasn't hysterical it was enigmatic:
John asks the students if any of them believed
in ghosts or spirits. No one said a word.
One shook his head slightly, no, no one else
shook anything at all.

I told a committee at an interview that poetry
could be a kind of stuttering. They lowered their heads in unison,
I lost the job. I believe
I would have lost the job anyway
but maybe my wife would have stood a chance.

Outside/within American and I assume cities of the world
there are Peep Shows, Adult World-s. Often
they are within firing range of a bus station, a train stop.
Often.

I am in love with the world tonight for I was sincere
when I threw my body against his to protect him in the bar
from what I feared
were gunshots. They were firecrackers, it was the 4th of July
in the Year of the Tall Ships, I had forgotten.
The bar was too empty to laugh.

There is a generous fire in my friend.
And he kept two finches and did not want them to die.
Of course when he was younger . . . like me in that anything could
die and it didn't matter, it did not die. If you went
to public school you would go to hell
but you would not die.

John's uncle, whose name I've misplaced: if anyone complimented
his attire he said something like "You like these shoes?
These shoes cost me fifty dollars."

Portrait

"If you change this I'll kill you."
—Mystery Novel

She smashed the portrait of herself.
Then she took a cutting knife
and locked herself in their bedroom.
She said she would not come out.

*

When I lie in the darkness unable to sleep
one eye attempts to locate the other eye.
I am without love.

The hotel is empty and it is summer.
If I listen closely I can hear bird songs almost all day.
Somehow, each day, I forget to listen this closely.

*

One of them moved to Cleveland.
One of them moved in July.
One of them left town, became a priest, and didn't tell anyone.
One of them said "I have never heard someone speak
    such singular feelings."

One of them said, "Father, no one but God knows how much
    hatred I have for myself."

*

Stories were her life.
Was the gash in her arm evidence of this?
The waterfall fell silently behind the glass.

She drove home. She wooed a man in white.
The rejected one saw an image of "the white one" in a film, years
ago, and spat.

Anima

I entered this house
with the man of the house.
I stood very awkwardly at the bottom of stairs
as he went here and there in the house.
A voice said I was responsible for
death. It was a woman's voice.

Two children now stood at the top of the stairs
with a woman in tow. Was this what I was here for,
these three,
who looked as awkward as I saw myself?

Is this what is a truer human knowledge,
knowledge or its possibility long after the ending,
far in another country,
—my heart isn't in this knowledge.

If this is when it arrives, years later,
I would rather it not arrive at all,
or arrive so late I have already departed
as one departs when the train is so overdue

one can't believe anyone.
And who wants to? For if one had sought belief
one would never have been here
in the first place.

Sun: go down.
Night: appear dark.
I do not appreciate having been so misled.

And if I have misled myself—
then let me reenter this house, awkwardly,
brutally, as a matter of fact.

A Raincoat

My mother kisses me goodnight for the thousandth time.
I am always wondering now, is this the last kiss?
Is this the end—for I have begun to see the face of an end
and it is not such a dark end, nor wholly white with light.
It is as if one will don a raincoat for a journey into eternity.
That is the most I can say about this face.
My mother's face—ahh! Now that I forgave myself I can see her
    face

and it is more beautiful now
than ever before in its seventy years.
And to think I worry about my face, and you
yours! How foolish.
My darling I told you my memory was forming in a central place
around a raincoat. And my young friend, whom I feuded with
as only friends will, walking to school with me in abject silence

(we were feuding but walking together!)

and my brother attempting to break the silence for us.
It broke, I know it broke, I don't know when and where
but yes it broke . . .

and did I tell you I might see death before any of us . . .
    and I say this
not to frighten us but to tell you it is alright, to tell myself
it is alright . . . it is believable

and death is so broke it needs us . . .
I believe the momentum of a life never, never stops . . .
the breath never ceases . . . the moon and the sycamore never
    cease to
miss us as we miss them . . .

A raincoat—I cannot even begin to articulate this coat . . .
the lives it saw, the leaves it saw orphaned at school,
the words like orphans which fell against the silent night
from a child's mouth. The breath of the closet like a stone filled
with light as the closet knew the moon or sun rose . . .

the paint which married one of its sleeves . . .
the coy view the raincoat possessed of my mother and my sister . . .
if this raincoat could have met you darling . . .

people's faces . . . in the square, in the school, in the window our
    souls
climbed at night when we slept in each other's arms . . . the faces
    at sea
accompanying the faces on the roads to the sea . . . the faces of your
sons and your daughter, my mother and father, the lost ones who
love us without our ever knowing . . . how constant they are

in this life and death which is one beauty . . .
Shhh! A child is hanging his raincoat . . . my mother
kisses us goodnight . . .

Shortage of Memory

The supposed map of the murderer's route
is the most detailed map of the country north
of here I've ever seen. There are arrows pointing
east from where the mailman lived
in Westernville to Wheelertown Road: 25 miles
to where his body was found.
There's a photograph of Streifert below the map
standing in a doorway in casual dress
drinking from what appears to be a coffee cup.

Time won't fail anyone:
I forgot the murder and went for a walk
down some side streets which reveal the backs
of the houses and contribute a different angle
on the steeples. When you drive into this town from the east
on the main road one of the first sights is 5 or 6
steeples. They are all the more clearer because 10 years ago
the town took most of the town down.
For night they've reignited the giant red figure of
Paul Revere galloping endlessly nowhere over the Revere Plant
which despite the reigniting of the man and horse
is closed.

I clocked my memory as taking a murdered road since 1966
or 20 years ago. Ignited by a turning in. An almost imperceptible
longing for north or cold: Buck Hill, the Town of Russia,
Black Hollow Road. I drove there to ignite the torch of my
memory and I did. I took it with me wherever
I went.

I don't remember anymore. Which is fine. I'm so sick of
    remembering
I'm not keeping this map to post: in my head, the car, a book, a
    box
so lacking in particulars the box would be the place for the map.
None of these places.

Singing in the Rain

Gogol (his namesake) answered the telephone. He met the
   woman—
a friend of a friend of a friend—downtown, to provide with
   housing information,
places to go, what to avoid in the city.

The rain fell like a lock from the sky—
they were drenched. They talked over coffee—
the conversation fell to silent places of her father's alcoholism.

Gogol told the little he knew
—he watched and listened from the tower of 'How come?"
the tower that simply regards life a little too severely.

When they parted he knew he would never see her again. The rain
still fell—he sang in the rain, at first
in a doorway, then on the street, hardly anyone could hear

the rain crowded everyone
and they dashed. Except for Gogol. Even lightning and thunder
didn't sway him. For Gogol this was unique.

*

"One lives in the hope of becoming a memory." (Antonio Porchia)
No. Uh-uh. Not anymore.
And Gogol's thinking of another writer: it's almost as if his friend's
   writing
depended upon meeting the friend. The writing is so flat you
   wonder if
there's a living breath behind it. Or a memory.

Gogol believes there are ghosts which bind us to them until
we accept them as our ghosts. These ghosts inhabit the city,
the desert, the mountains, the seas—anywhere where any of these
are. When you meet one in the city as Gogol did you are not
   alarmed.
Even if the initial moment of the voice is the telephone and you are
   nervous.

The Size of One's Hand

I know I gave everything I could—the literal objects
which possessed any identity I placed in objects—
a basket secretly made in the woods,
the size of one's hand,
a painting done almost by accident
which captures tentativeness, warning.

One other bride to cross and I cannot cross her,
one other road away from the same self.
I have fled, I am broken.

The last rain is not even falling in the trees.
It is not out nor in.
It is far—
far beyond even the horizon I give my hand to.

I am living and I am dead.
As empty as a bridge only
one moment after rain.

Small Moment

My friend said I love the snow
on that yellow house. Flora had a house like that, in another life,
                    with fake lions in front.

        26
people congregate
                    in the photograph:
they are bleached by the sunlight,
they look as if they are waiting for cash.
One of the women

                    is so ancient now she wishes she were
        the photograph itself,

not as she appeared
but the thing itself.
She told me so. She also told me

the photograph was taken in 1935
and she is 30 years off.

                    *

                    My lover is more than my lover.
                    My lover
                        asks where do your parents
really
            come from.
        My father
held a flashlight to his face two rooms away,
my mother told me to look. I looked.
It was very peculiar: he had a hat on, a flashlight beneath his chin,

his smile
was exaggerated. I do not know where they come from
    but I know this:

this is one of 3 or 4 most remarkable incidents in my life,
very small moments, moments in another life I may overlook.
Another one involved the two of them,

in a house by the sea, laughing and crying then
at the same time, one became the other,
as he told me about his father in a house

                                   by the sea.
                Another: it is late

to be still
with this
another couple: we have driven: we are it seems literally going
   nowhere.

         I have bent down with a bottle to help them
with their water
and the moon is just so

—haven't even noticed it. Then its full light
is upon my hands as the water from the spring is upon my hands,
   I am alone
as their car has moved

and they are trotting down the road to stop it.
It is such a small moment the world has ended,

I don't even try to make it last.

Someone of Us

It could have been any one of us driving to the obscure:
Everyone had died at once,
I had a tendency to rewrite my past, and among the forests
I found others like this too.

So I was not alone, nor were they.
There was still some feeling climbing away from us
which injured our history, but the injury wasn't enough.
Not enough to make us stop or begin again only
    on its own account.

When she suffered I suffered.
When I drew water from the sea
she drew also, sometimes pieces of night
from a night sky, but still a drawing from.

If the forest moaned in the wind
we heard it as a momentary sign,
we didn't shudder or fear.
If the forest moaned in the night we were less certain

but still able to ascertain some distance between us
and it. And then the day came when someone of us whispered
that the soul was an illusion anyway, and another one of us
invited phantoms to come and live

—it was within these contradictions
where everything made sense again:
the first was both the first and the last
the last a feeling we had already suffered.

Third Autumn

Reading Anna K—
but skipping Levin's story
after page 238
until he meets Anna.

Convinced van Gogh read
similarly—
no . . .

for two autumns
I attempted Anna Karenina:
1980, 1984. Inexplicable
loneliness took over,
didn't draw
a plausible thread between the two
until:

now, 1985,
third autumn.

Ghostly inability
to stop thinking of Anna.
"Know" the end—
not through my own reading

but through general or overheard
discussions of it,
the end. Her end.

100 pages to go.
Bus, bus station.
"Elaine Barkow"
called upon paging-phone.
German, she says,
to the mom beside her.
Ticket as far as Dover.

Tonight will sleep
with its leg outside the sheet
so someone may sleep upon it
if they want.

As for A.K.:
have this ghostly feeling
her end will approximate mine,
or vice versa.

So be it:
love you beyond any palpable belief,
have meant to utter that
for almost a year
in a letter
which was never sent.

The bus is full.
Weak with the night
and the inexplicable
Elaine Barkow.

3-Part-Fire

moon waned
like cold brick

do not reach far
across your love

do not sell
what cannot be sold

return to all goods:
stone, first jewels, early

promise of a bell
to satisfy the branch

in the child: first
lesson: 3-part-fire

will in turn make each
loved one huddle together

in the distant past as
strangers shone

in the windows of the
stranded but well-lit train

Two Faces

The difference remains in each, and so bounds them.
Not unlike how differently they will cross the road, the sea, the
    death

between the mountain and sea
if the death shall find them.

When she was old she got out of the sleigh
and watched the blue snow fall upon the yellow house

before walking into the house. A man too far away to see clearly
was calling to someone beyond himself, up the street

which led to the park
which was empty on the snowy evening.

When one face has turned toward the park
another face follows it, the voice ahead

is followed by a voice behind, a few moments later a bell tingles,
someone is now asleep and someone else is gazing at the town

and the night for a loved one. Almost anyone will do.
When two faces have met for as long as a winter

differences begin to act wildly upon the faces: one is one, one
is

the other, though they know this isn't true. The boundary of night
is true, and they long for it.

2 Poems on the Same Theme

Unlike my friend John I like the painting entitled
Biography: it is a little one-sided with primitivism
but I forgive it that. Still, I've always been
haunted by John's silence about this one, an absolute
silence. A student says the painting was stolen
from his own idea: and I am wondering if mentioning
this could be construed as another steal: the snow
is falling—stolen: the song the parakeet is
chirping is for all I know stolen, stolen among
numerous songs which have passed cage to cage,
gene to gene, without anyone calling thief.
Bags of stone are beside the railroad bridge, the
train is standing still waiting for the workers
to clear from the bridge: a light snow is falling
in the painting: the workers have dots for eyes:
near another bag of stone the woman still walks
along, offended years later still by the death on
her way to her wedding. The husband-to-be and the
parents of the long-awaiting-bride stolen from her
in a foreign country, Germany I think. Or so the
story goes. She goes, the painting goes, the weak
like me forget it and drive into the country.
John is dreaming we've boarded the train again,
dreaming who will get off first, and where, when.

*

My friend John has
never said a peep about
my poem Biography. A
student of mine says
I stole it from her.
I received a registered
piece of me guaranteeing
I hear her opening argument
and another letter later.
I did not answer this
latter letter. I thought

I tried stealing a tone
from Montale, or how I
heard him. The biography
the student says was
Modigliani, the subject
of mine is female. This
is beginning to sound like
a hollow offense. John's
silence feels like a key
to a refrain of silence:
so I am looking at a
reproduction of Grandma
Moses' In the Park, the
obvious silence of the couple
about to cross the covered
bridge on foot, and the eternal
silence of the river and
the house above the couple
and the river. I wish I
were dreaming of John and
me boarding a train again,
who would get off first,
where, when. And I am
wondering this Christmas
morning in 1985 what the
walker in Clinton, New York
is doing: the story goes
her husband-to-be and
her parents disembarked
for death the day of
her wedding in a foreign
country, Germany I think.
I tried writing about her
twice, a poem called
Moonlike Leaf and another
called Out There. Neither
addressed her fully.

silencing the moon

do not drift with them
who do and shall and always will /
there is an ended time from childhood
when the first tale of burial is heard and disbelieved:

this tale is for those locked in time and space
which only the eerie evening can detect and murmur to /
shadow of the unbeliever shining through the cartwheel
and another hole of evening permitting

the echo of reverie to repeat itself in the dead condition
    of a memory
silencing the moon and turning far away when
the first stars make their accurate appearance

—someone with a cap hung on their skull has carried the
    bucket of evening
back from the well—the river has mended again
and no one thinks twice with feeling

—someone with a cap hung on their skull has carried the
    bucket of evening
back from the well—a solstice with a dark hole at its center
breathes an apogee no one smells

—he doesn't smell permission and thus he and they continue
begging from a childhood cruelty without even knowing
they are asking

A Walk at Chicago

Jack, do you have a brother in Albany? If so
he is working for the train.

The heart is a brown eye across the countryside. He wanted to tell
    you
the people in the landscapes appear awkward and flattened

        because they are,
because there is a sense that they do not belong,

we have never belonged, but are allowed here   as long as we
    accept
this status of awkwardness. The eyes look like raisins and
    periodically

like flies, they may represent a fear of making mistakes
                (mistaking dark trees on the hill

    for the god hour, the woman beside you
for the village of Rotterdam, the river between the two trees as a
    river which moves
nowhere ceaselessly). The eyes may also represent

a location somewhere between the present and the past,
a latitude which is equally neither, asking like an old voice

what is the alternative?
what does messenger mean? At night

late beyond most people an odd confidence glows against the sky,
it can hardly be seen with the naked eye but it is there, it is felt,

the stars are showing off against the sea, the pieces of ice
in a harbor almost seem to have a heart. Your brother is breathing.

He wanted to tell you there are people in darkness against the
    heart.

A Star, a Loan

there is one moment and there is the next: and rain:
the sound of the rain—I want to color it, give it something back
pale as it has given so much to me:

I want to describe memory, memory since I have been in your arms:
now it is no longer an organization:

it is: a star, a loan,
a secret cave: the fact of it:
inside I feel it, as if it is now a spatial dimension, a crow
across the world, a wind there:

fact of: place /
time / harmony / people /

it has somehow come within me, as something almost dear:
have never actually believed in a ghost—is this how the ghost

would feel?
Since your kiss has fallen my way
I have little to say anymore:

"anymore"—that is a sound of the rain.
There seems to be one moment when all of the rain I hear is a
    moment
between drops:

Jo Ann's mad uncle is climbing down the stairs because it is raining
Jo Ann is climbing out the window because her mad uncle is
    climbing down the stairs

/ I am between the door and the glass
and I am listening to rain

Wanted

I could give you:
the donkey of whom I am afraid.
The man who wears his jacket forever, outside, inside.
The hill I climb when the stars are you.

I could take the pieces of every horse which has died from a beating
and make a story from them, or a sun, or a pistol
which could shoot only beaters.
And I could remind you that one hundred souls applauded
    when we met.

I heard them in the spoon.
I heard them in the tree.
You heard them in our train which called to us,
and in the rain which was a queen.

I have no associations tonight beyond these,
because I am without you.
Because the day ended as it began
without you.

Today I passed the creek I was lowered from by youthful thugs
    when I was young.
The drop seemed then forever.
A boy was fishing from the bridge, the drop is only about 4 feet
if you are hung from the bridge as I was.

I stalled them with a plea I would give them something of mine
    from home,
I believe I offered them my comic books if they let me go.
They did, I never returned, I never saw them again.
And for someone so intimidated it is a miracle I passed the creek
    again.

I had to. The creek crossing was the route to school.
School was truly about something else, some other
    condition suspended
from the branch of life, a condition only alluded to,
never made clear. The motorcycle cop I worshipped

now to my memory looks like a crime, a factor from a world war,
the dark glasses he always wore make me think of cobras,
although cobras and glasses do not look alike.
God, that street feels cold.

What I am getting at is
the route to school was the route to God,
no one told us so.
It has taken me this long just to begin understanding.

God is not what they told us.
God is this invisible membrane which keeps me with you.
Of course saying so I know I violate—for words don't know,
I don't know.

I sense this invisibility yet it is incomprehensible.
So was the night we met.
Incomprehensible.
I always wanted poems to talk to an incomprehensible state,

there for a sense of being but always, how do you say,
 about slightly something else.
Not symbolism, more like a painting with words.
Here a face with an eye missing, thee a name mistakenly called—
left to remain a name as thee came from beyond me.

Life is a gift.
I wanted this gift to be given. I wanted to write a poem
which would talk to you only,
to tell you where I have been.

The Secret

The sun knew it: birds think.
Then why did your bones choose white?

I know, I know: I am putting off facing
the shore of my secret.
If I let myself see it . . .

I did not even know there was a secret
until you said there must be . . .

My mother: I am responsible for my mother because
I found her making love to a bird . . .

I am not trying to make light of this,
I am trying to approach:

My father, my, my, my:
I smashed the possession called his watch and hid it.

I lied, so the final confession was doubled.
Upon that day I earned the word "my" . . .

Endings, there must be endings,
I do not even know what I mean . . .

I mean: if birds do think then someone knows,
someone has seen this secret,

someone other that my self owns this,
birds, bones, sun: what do my bones know,

did they give me intuition in exchange for the secret?
And her, my love, how does she know?

The sun must have known her in my life
before I did . . .

The secret is: my mother is on a stairwell
—I am far away in a name

—the name is not mine
for I was never conceived with a name.

I was dropped into their life
like the night drops light sometimes

and makes you feel as if you have been
washed with an innocence unlike

human innocence.
The child before me is now falling

with my mother.
They will not tell you now

but you have been blamed.
You will attempt to repeat the act:

kicking your sister down a stairwell.
She will not die or be scarred,

but I will carry a scar for doing this.
I came to this secret like

an accident. I knew from the womb
I was to blame for my brother's death,

death before me. Someone
to silently blame.

The White Door

If your teeth are crooked
God will straighten them,
or God will provide you
with braces. The braces of the sky
have been provided by silos:

and in winter a character
whose demise is more like the demise
of a gaslamp than a human demise,
more a flame condescended to
as the author struggles to prevent
too much

sympathy for death by her own
neck, for death which is sustained
as a mild hysteria, a mistake,
the white door in a dream minutes
before waking for the day, day of
the red door and, mother, farewell.

The White Moon Night

I used to die in my memory,
a blackbird sweetened the death
by flying with me.

O my god
the moon is a sea again
beyond the three houses and the bridge.

All my life I've been looking for someone.
I have met the someone more than once.
I am poor for I have lost someone.

In the first house there is a lunar table.
A painting of a pursuer.
An indefinable history which portrays love.

My memory is your kiss.
Too many men of the world are arming against the world.
We do not matter to them.

In your kiss there is a still lunar bird.
A white wing, a red wing.
Voices which belong to your first children.

A hatred of school is a love of memory.
The school is the tardy one.
Someone who also hated school is telephoning from
    a thousand miles away.

The men against the world are against the sea also.
A love of history is a hatred of tides.
An umbrella cracks against the pavement.

The rain falls making the leaves such dead things
the mind turns away. Fortunately for the leaves
they do not depend upon the mind.

I have mailed my stone to your sister.
A gift which will arrive too late to save you,
to save me, to save us against the white moon night.

If there were more possibilities they would state me.
This estrangement is like an iron tongue.
The bells chime hourly in the sun of the tower

—and at night, when no one cares to hear them, I ask them
to transport the beating of a heart, a drop of rain, a light
from this world to this world.

I ask the night to have a heart,
a small word or two, a mouth
to speak to you from and two lips to kiss you.

$$\frac{86}{87}$$

Afterword

I wrote many of these poems while literally in motion. I was busing and training back and forth between Salisbury, Maryland, and Rome, New York in the winter and spring and then summer of 1986. I had a "silent" typewriter and began to feel motion was good for my writing. At one point, after having written a great deal, for better or worse, in 1984 and 1985, and early 1986, I tried to see if I could imagine a voice talking texts of poems. I wanted to hear a woman's voice. I called the voice "Katya." It was a Russian voice. I thought this would be very self-conscious and maybe preposterous, but I also thought my sincerity might help. I believe in poems often being overheard from voices in the outside world, or imagined voices, or collages of these.

Some of the poems from this same time appear in *Fictions from the Self* or *The Fires They Kept*, and (a few more) in *Entire Dilemma*. Some of the poems ("Amends," "my brother dreams") were not recopied for a few years. Maybe I had no faith in them. At the same time, I did not want to break up the manuscript they were in, even though I composed many tables of contents for what eventually became *Entire Dilemma*.

Many of the poems in *Pennsylvania Collection Agency* were centered in relationships which formed or revisited themselves during that time. Central to these were a relationship with Nancy Mitchell, with her children, Zac and Sara and Seth; a relationship with my parents whom I unexpectedly lived with while I taught at Syracuse University in the winter/spring of 1986; relationships with old and new friends, some "writing" friends—John Skoyles, Jean Valentine, Maria Flook—some not—Mary Hackett, Bill Bronson; childhood friends like Rusty Grove ("A Raincoat"), acquaintances from childhood, Butchie Stevenson ("Each of Them Icons"). And relatives alive and well and some newly deceased. Neighbors, alive and dead. Sometimes my sister and my brother were fictive in their "roles" in poems as to detail but not to emotional fact. Sometimes when I look back at these poems, or actually read them, I fear they sound like they are looking through only a few emotional windows. Then at other times I get a sense that is not true at all—and I am surprised at how many windows seem to be in them.

"Amends." Maybe that is now what in part these poems are trying to do. To make amends. Perhaps there was/is some unseen reason they stayed together like this as a manuscript until now. Maybe I could not really look until now.

The silences in my family both imprisoned me and made me turn to the prisons and freedoms of words. They created secrets which could harm me because I did not know what to do with what was not being said—with what I could only sense, not say (and perhaps be "doomed" to the task of trying to say—who knows). But they also created much room. Many rooms to roam in. To look out from. To wonder from.

"Amends" was written in what struck me as a flat voice after Nancy had had me drive her to a school where she taught. Like many of these poems, this poem seemed to write itself. Motion sponsored this poem as well.

The title poem is from a sign I saw from a bus when I was in downtown Philadelphia. I was looking out in order to look in. I was looking in in order to look out. I think my poems see things more clearly than I see them, or they come closer to saying what I see.

There are so many people involved in my writing of these poems I am not sure I could mention them all, but I probably could. What is behind the poems is as important for me to talk about as the poems themselves. Circumstances. A life. Lives. This is what writes the poems at best. When "I" enters too narrowly I think something collapses very quickly, even if briefly.

I wrote a number of the poems in this book in the "presence" of my mother and father. I would be typing on my silent electronic typewriter and they would be moving about the house. I wrote in the dining room. Sometimes I wrote "immediately" to concerns in the literal present moment: "my brother dreams" written during the time of my Aunt Lelia's death and wake; "A Raincoat" came one night, after my mother came in to kiss me goodnight. I went back to my reading, but wondered how many more times she would be able to kiss me goodnight.

My mother was suffering from Alzheimer's—but I thought it was like my alcoholism—it seemed a disease of denial. Now, in hindsight, I can see there were many little things that could have given her away, but didn't, for whatever reason. Of course, this contributed to silences. My father, despite a continuing zeal for music—piano, organ—had suffered from poor hearing for many years. A certain kind of intimate conversation was difficult, if only for tone's sake. And then if you take into account how members of my family didn't seem interested in the same conversation I was interested in, about the past, and how I accentuated this too much, well, that tension, those tensions, led to poems too.

I am surprised I was writing around my parents so literally. "Each of Them Icons," "My Mother Orders a Children's Book," "Shortage of Memory" (the morning after the news report).

On the train I would write "A Walk at Chicago," "Moon to a Far Planet," a few of the Katya poems ("Sober Ghost"—"Katya"—which is in *Entire Dilemma*). It was as if the motion of travel was freeing me, or putting me in touch with something I very much needed/wanted to hear while being at "home" with my parents—which used to create a standstill (certainly for my writing—I never wrote when visiting them until a little bit in 1978, and only a little after that). So being home allowed me to write about past homes, houses, the house of 907 (907 was the address of a favorite house we had lived in in Rome, New York, until I was nine. But it was also the street number of the house I got sober in, in Salisbury, Maryland, in 1982. 907 Croton Street. 907 North Division.)

Lisa Bateman, Tamara Kennelley, Tom Lindsay, Elizabeth Mott, Carl Hughes. "Elaine Barkow." Marsha. It's as if all those behind and to the side of these poems inform them. And something about being with Nancy Mitchell and my being with my family again—unexpectedly, unplanned—something about being in the orbits of those dear to me—allows me to overhear. It is hard to talk about. Or it slips away.

Even a dear friend from my high school past, Rose Gulla DeAngelo, comes back into my life unexpectedly in the summer/fall. Almost as if she sets a stage to leave a writing life behind for the time being, as if I am brought up to the present moment now in a different sense—and by the late fall of 1986 I am writing less. I am drawing. I am drawing more. The last couple of poems in this book in terms of when they were written are "A Raincoat" and "A White Moon Night." The earliest is "Amends." Maybe some orbit is drawn down. Or I am written out until I begin keeping a journal in the summer of 1987. Which becomes *My Secret Boat*. Poems outside of that—until 1990—take on a tone I can't locate as well or recognize as well. It's as if some kind of information stopped for the time being, as if it had to. Or I closed up.

—This seems far away.

Sober friends were connections for poems, too. And simply friends. Jane Boissy, her son—Clay Eichelberger, Charlie Bagley, Michael Waters, Robin; friend from the past, Jo Ann Marullo.

In 1981, after, for very sound reasons, not being able to write a blurb for my book *Ruby for Grief*, Tomas Tranströmer wrote to me in a letter about those poems: "in them, some ghost is operating too."

I wonder now if I was allowing the ghosts to operate even more so in *Pennsylvania Collection Agency*; if I was letting the information from the ghosts become more clearly a part of the poems, or a part of their faces. It occurs to me now, years later . . .

This sense that the information of the ghosts is active, present, not something from a past moment but current. Ghosts are not ghosts of the past but ghosts for, or of, the present.

—Michael Burkard

$$\frac{92}{93}$$

Acknowledgements

Grateful acknowledgement is made to the editors of the following
journals, magazines and anthologies in which these poems first
appeared, some in slightly different versions:

Agni Review: "Two Faces"
The American Poetry Review: "Because," "To Maria,"
     "2 Poems on the Same Theme," "The White Moon Night"
Blur: "Portrait," "How Much of the Life"
Burning Car: "Someone of Us"
Epoch: "Pennsylvania Collection Agency," "Hotel Tropicana"
The Iowa Review: "Each of Them Icons," "January 24, 1986 (moonset)"
Ironwood: "Nijinsky," "A Raincoat"
jubilat: "What I Threw Into the Grave"
Panoply: "The Size of One's Hand"
Provincetown Arts: "Moon to a Far Planet"
Salmon: "Amends"
Southern Poetry Review: "My Mother Orders a Children's Book,"
     "Shortage of Memory"
St. Andrews Review: "Her Healing," "The Pictures of Maria," "Anima"
Thinker Review: "Small Moment"
Volt: "It Is Quite Red" "The White Door"
Willow Springs: "Singing in the Rain," "Wanted"

"Hotel Tropicana" also appeared in *The Best American Poetry,*
1989 (Donald Hall editor, David Lehman Series Editor)
(Charles Scribner's Son's)

"A Raincoat" also appeared in *The Clinton Courier*, and in the
anthologies *First Light: Mother & Son Poems, A Twentieth-Century
Selection*, edited by Jason Shinder (Harcourt Brace Jovanovich,
New York, 1992) and *A Saratoga Anthology* (edited by Linda Bullard,
Saratoga Springs Public Library, 1996)

"Two Poems on the Same Theme" also appeared in *The Body Electric: The Best from the American Poetry Review*, 1972-1999 (edited by Stephen Berg, David Bonanno, and Arthur Vogelsang) (W.W. Norton & Company, 2000)

Samuel Charters' translation of Tomas Tranströmer's "The Blue House" appears in *Tomas Tranströmer, Selected Poems 1954-1986*, edited by Robert Hass. (The Ecco Press, New York, 1987).

I would like to thank the National Endowment for the Arts for a grant in 1985 during which time some of these poems were written.

A special thanks to Michael Gervasio, and to Keith Althaus and Susan Baker.

photo by jam

Michael Burkard's most recent collections of poetry are
Entire Dilemma (1998) and *Unsleeping* (2000), both from
Sarabande. He has received a Whiting Writers' Award, the
Poetry Society of America's Alice Fay di Castagnola Award,
and grants from the New York State Foundation for the Arts
and the National Endowment for the Arts. He currently
teaches at Syracuse University and at the Fine Arts Work
Center in Provincetown.

New Issues Poetry & Prose

Editor, Herbert Scott

James Armstrong, *Monument in a Summer Hat*
Michael Burkard, *Pennsylvania Collection Agency*
Anthony Butts, *Fifth Season*
Gladys Cardiff, *A Bare Unpainted Table*
Lisa Fishman, *The Deep Heart's Core Is a Suitcase*
Joseph Featherstone, *Brace's Cove*
Robert Grunst, *The Smallest Bird in North America*
Mark Halperin, *Time as Distance*
Myronn Hardy, *Approaching the Center*
Edward Haworth Hoeppner, *Rain Through High Windows*
Janet Kauffman, *Rot* (fiction)
Josie Kearns, *New Numbers*
Maurice Kilwein Guevara, *Autobiography of So-and-so:
    Poems in Prose*
Lance Larsen, *Erasable Walls*
David Dodd Lee, *Downsides of Fish Culture*
Deanne Lundin, *The Ginseng Hunter's Notebook*
Joy Manesiotis, *They Sing to Her Bones*
David Marlatt, *A Hog Slaughtering Woman*
Paula McLain, *Less of Her*
Malena Mörling, *Ocean Avenue*
Julie Moulds, *The Woman with a Cubed Head*
Marsha de la O, *Black Hope*
C. Mikal Oness, *Water Becomes Bone*
Elizabeth Powell, *The Republic of Self*
Margaret Rabb, *Granite Dives*
Rebecca Reynolds, *Daughter of the Hangnail*
Martha Rhodes, *Perfect Disappearance*
John Rybicki, *Traveling at High Speeds*
Mark Scott, *Tactile Values*
Diane Seuss-Brakeman, *It Blows You Hollow*
Marc Sheehan, *Greatest Hits*
Phillip Sterling, *Mutual Shores*
Angela Sorby, *Distance Learning*
Russell Thorburn, *Approximate Desire*
Robert VanderMolen, *Breath*
Martin Walls, *Small Human Detail in Care of National Trust*
Patricia Jabbeh Wesley, *Before the Palm Could Bloom:
    Poems of Africa*